MONTHLY GOAL WORKBOOK

Workbook to achieve one goal in one month

Your name:

Starting date:

GOAL FOR THIS MONTH:

www.spanishthinkingcoach.com

Dedicated to my parents,

Juan María and María Victoria.

Genius is one percent inspiration and ninety-nine percent perspiration. **Thomas A. Edison**

Index   Page

1. Guide

I enjoy thinking and generating ideas… but what is the point of having ideas unless you implement them?

When I wrote my two previous workbooks to ideas and inventions, I realised when I used them how much I needed them. The workbook I am presenting now follows that same path of helping me becoming more effective.

Before writing a book I have been a lot of time thinking about it, and for the time I force myself to sit down and write it, many of the ideas have been forgotten and they come once the book is already written. But still, it is better to have written something that later I can improve than no to have written anything.

Since I was a teenager I used to read books about personal development, in which you can think about what you want in life, your vision or your mission in life, so that you can make it achievable by planning the things in 10, 5 or 1 year. On many occasions it is not easy to know what you want to be or to do in the future (especially when you are a young person).

Even when you know more or less what you want to achieve in the long term, this ideas can change. I have focused in one month goal, because it is not too long time to loose motivation and it is enough time to achieve valuable results (you could paint a house, learn coding, write a book, change habits, make friends, etc.) or at least to have given a big push to something that make it easier to continue with it.

I have found that there are very structured processes to achieve goals, advice that can motivate you (food for thought), some activities that can help you with it, tips for specific issues (health, etc.).

Before anything, you need to be motivated to achieve one goal. Sometimes, it can help thinking about people that already have achieved it, visualising yourself doing it, remembering goals that you have already achieved recently so that it seems similarly achievable, and asking yourself questions about what you want to achieve and why.

The key to start anything is to make it easy. Even before making it easy you have to decide exactly what is what you really want to achieve, what motivates you. This needs to be thought properly, as we can have different ways of dealing with issues by achieving different type of goals. It is like when you have a problem and there are different ways of dealing with it. First you have to choose the way that is better for you according to your knowledge, experience and motivation.

The monthly objective must be helped by a long term framework and a shorter time support. We are going to talk about a VISION (life time), in 5 to 10 years, in one year, in one month, in one week and in one day (and even here and now…how do you feel?).

The long term is not easy to identify, but it is interesting to think about it. We could ask ourselves questions such as "What would I do if I won the lottery (1,000.000.000)?", "What would I do if I had a terminal illness?", "what I am good at?", "What I like doing?", "What would I like to improve in the world or in my community?", "What I would like to help with?". When I was a teenager, I did not know what to answer to these questions. I was not sure even what I wanted to study… so my answer was to continue thinking about it, search information, try things to see what I like more, what I am good at, finding new things to do, volunteering, helping others, etc.

It is easier to think about what you are going to do in the next 1 to 5 years. Maybe you are thinking about studies, career change, change of employment, buying a house, doing business, savings, health, etc.

MY FOCUS: 1 MONTH

As I said before my favourite time frame is one month because it allows me time to achieve important things and at the same time I can deal with my other commitments and keep motivated as it is just 4 weeks (or 4 weekends) to achieve it.

Weekly timetable
This is a very good tool to write what are your commitments (work, studies, etc.), appointments, etc. and see the gaps where you can fit activities to achieve what you want and to balance your timetable (physical, mental, social). It does not matter if one week you are 100 per cent committed to your goal, but as a healthy habit, you should also do other type of activities to make a healthy routine that will help you with your goal achievement.

Daily to do list.
Besides the weekly timetable, every day you can adjust your day, looking at new things to do, things to leave for another day, miscellaneous, etc. and thinking about the time when to do them. When doing the "Daily to do list" and the "Weekly timetable" it is important to remember the monthly goal, as the monthly goal might seem not as urgent as other daily things, but the achievement of the monthly goal can have a greater impact on our lives.

The monthly objective is important because it allows you to do important things, productive activities, to build something, to become something.

When you do something, when you make something or build something, you realise that you have skills, value. If you don´t do things like this in a while you might loose confidence on your ability to use these skills. Besides, when doing things, you rediscover yourself, remembering what things you like doing and what you believe you are good at or in which activity your could excel.

"We are what we repeatedly do. Excellence, then, is not an act, but a habit." Aristotle

2. Vision and goals after 5 years

<u>VISION (life time goals)</u>

<u>Goals after 5 years</u>

3. Goals 1 – 5 years

4. Goals for this year

5. This month calendar

Here you can write any important events during the month and circle in red the weekends and bank holidays.

1

2

3

4

5

6

7

8

9

10

11

12

13

14

15

16

17

18

19

20

21

22

23

24

25

26

27

28

29

30

31

6. Goal for this month

Which goal with produce more impact on my life and I am more enthusiastic about?

WHY IS THIS GOAL SO IMPORTANT?

7. Weekly plans (to do at the beginning of the month and every Sunday)

In this weekly plans you can write your commitments as well as the time (inside the same cell or on the left). As the page is small you could do it in another piece of paper so you have more space to write.

I have included two more weeks because the month could start at any time. You should write the number of the day. For example, if the month starts on Friday:

Time	Mon	Tuesd	Wedne	Thur	Friday	Sat.	Sund
					1	2	3

And continue with the following weeks:

Time	Mon	Tuesd	Wedne	Thur	Friday	Sat.	Sund
	4	5	6	7	8	9	10

Time	Mon	Tuesd	Wedne	Thur	Friday	Sat.	Sund
	11	12	13	14	15	16	17

Time	Mon	Tuesd	Wedne	Thur	Friday	Sat.	Sund
	18	19	20	21	22	23	24

Time	Mon	Tuesd	Wedne	Thur	Friday	Sat.	Sund
	25	26	27	28	29	30	31

1ST WEEK OBJECTIVES / PLAN

You can write some activities at the beginning of the month and update them every Sunday before the following week to adjust it. When you have written your appointments, you can see the gaps and add the other activities you want to do achieve your monthly goal and to be balanced.

Time	Mon	Tuesd	Wedne	Thur	Friday	Sat.	Sund

On Sunday you can think about how the planning was and what was achieved and do adjustments for next week.

2nd WEEK OBJECTIVES / PLAN

Time	Mon	Tuesd	Wedne	Thur	Friday	Sat.	Sund

3rd WEEK OBJECTIVES / PLAN

Time	Mon	Tuesd	Wedne	Thur	Friday	Sat.	Sund

4th WEEK OBJECTIVES / PLAN

Time	Mon	Tuesd	Wedne	Thur	Friday	Sat.	Sund

5th WEEK OBJECTIVES / PLAN

Time	Mon	Tuesd	Wedne	Thur	Friday	Sat.	Sund

6th WEEK OBJECTIVES / PLAN

Time	Mon	Tuesd	Wedne	Thur	Friday	Sat.	Sund

8. Example "TO DO" list (to do the night before)

List "Things to be done today". You can organise by priorities
(first what is more urgent) or by time.   This is an example, as
also you can write it in another paper that you can carry
during the day to remember what to do and when.

Priority	To do
1	
2	
3	
4	
Etc.	

Time	To do
9.00-10.00	
10.00-11-00	
11.00-12.30	
12.30-15.00	
Etc.	

9. Daily reminders (to keep motivated)

Things I am proud to have achieved are…

I am good at…

I feel grateful for…

The activities I enjoy more during the day and during the week are…

Things I would like to do or to learn are…

10. Daily questions (to keep thinking daily)

MORNING
What are my vision, long term goals, 1 year goals?
What do I want to achieve today?
How can I enjoy doing it?

½ DAY
How is the day so far?
What is left to be done?
Do I need to adjust the daily "TO DO" list and postpone
something or do something today supposed to be done
tomorrow or other day?

EVENING
What went well today?
How do I feel about the day? What did I use the time for?
What could I do different for next time?
What can I do to balance the type of activities I have done
today?

11.Daily records

Daily records can be used to write the list of things to be done next day, but especially the main idea it is to write a reflection of the day.   A reflective practice in which you can answer questions like the ones shown in the EVENING daily questions. This will give the opportunity to monitor how we are doing and to think what needs to be done to achieve the monthly goal.

I have left some blank pages so you can have some room to start the week from Monday even if the first day of the month is on any other day.

DAY

DAY

DAY

DAY

DAY

DAY

DAY 1

DAY 2

DAY 3

DAY 4

DAY 5

DAY 6

DAY 7

DAY 8

DAY 9

DAY 10

DAY 11

DAY 12

DAY 13

DAY 14

DAY 15

DAY 16

DAY 17

DAY 18

DAY 19

DAY 20

DAY 21

DAY 22

DAY 23

DAY 24

DAY 25

DAY 26

DAY 27

DAY 28

DAY 29

DAY 30

DAY 31

DAY

DAY

DAY

DAY

DAY

DAY

12. Inspiring quotations

Successful weight loss takes programming, not willpower.
Phil McGraw

We are what we repeatedly do. Excellence, then, is not an act, but a habit.
Aristotle

Education is the methodical creation of the habit of thinking.
Ernest Dimnet

Without struggle, no progress and no result. Every breaking of habit produces a change in the machine.
George Gurdjieff

"Watch your thoughts; they become words. Watch your words; they become actions. Watch your actions; they become habit. Watch your habits; they become character. Watch your character; it becomes your destiny."
 Lao Tzu

How wonderful it is that nobody need wait a single moment before starting to improve the world.
Anne Frank

What you get by achieving your goals is not as important as what you become by achieving your goals.
Henry David Thoreau

People are not lazy. They simply have impotent goals - that is, goals that do not inspire them.
Tony Robbins

One reason so few of us achieve what we truly want is that we never direct our focus; we never concentrate our power. Most people dabble their way through life, never deciding to master anything in particular.
Tony Robbins

See yourself how you want to be 5 years from now and start acting like that person TODAY. Fiona Harrold

The question is not 'Who am I?' but 'Who do I want to be?'
Fiona Harrold

Eighty percent of all choices are based on fear. Most people don't choose what they want; they choose what they think is safe.
Phil McGraw

The Internet is just bringing all kinds of information into the home. There's just a lot of distraction, a lot of competition for the parent's voice to resonate in the children's ears.
Phil McGraw

It's hard to see your own face without a mirror.
Phil McGraw

A goal is a dream with a deadline.
Napoleon Hill

It is not enough to take steps which may some day lead to a goal; each step must be itself a goal and a step likewise.
Johann Wolfgang von Goethe

There are two things to aim at in life; first to get what you want, and after that to enjoy it. Only the wisest of mankind has achieved the second.
Logan Pearsall Smith

Procrastination is like a credit card: it's a lot of fun until you get the bill.
Christopher Parker

Better three hours too soon, than one minute too late.
William Shakespeare

Don't be fooled by the calendar. There are only as many days in the year as you make use of. One man gets only a week's value out of a year while another man gets a full year's value out of a week.
Charles Richards

The key is in not spending time, but in investing it.
Stephen R. Covey

If you want to make good use of your time, you've got to know what's most important and then give it all you've got.
Lee Iacocca

It's not enough to be busy, so are the ants. The question is, what are we busy about?
Henry David Thoreau

Don't say you don't have enough time. You have exactly the same number of hours per day that were given to Helen Keller, Pasteur, Michelangelo, Mother Teresa, Leonardo da Vinci, Thomas Jefferson, and Albert Einstein.

There are three constants in life... change, choice and principles.
Stephen Covey

The key is taking responsibility and initiative, deciding what your life is about and prioritizing your life around the most important things.
Stephen Covey

We are the creative force of our life, and through our own decisions rather than our conditions, if we carefully learn to do certain things, we can accomplish those goals.
Stephen Covey

All successful people men and women are big dreamers. They imagine what their future could be, ideal in every respect, and then they work every day toward their distant vision, that goal or purpose.
Brian Tracy

Your vision will become clear only when you can look into your own heart. Who looks outside, dreams; who looks inside, awakes.
Carl Jung

Good business leaders create a vision, articulate the vision, passionately own the vision, and relentlessly drive it to completion.
Jack Welch

Each of us has a vision of good and of evil. We have to encourage people to move towards what they think is good... Everyone has his own idea of good and evil and must choose to follow the good and fight evil as he conceives them. That would be enough to make the world a better place.
Pope Francis

Failing to plan is planning to fail.
Alan Lakein

If you always do what you've always done, you'll always get what you've always got." Henry Ford

A designer is someone who constructs while he thinks, someone for whom planning and making go together.
John Maeda

You can continue adding more quotations or your own thoughts:

You can find my other books and resources in my websites:

www.spanishthinkingcoach.com

www.learningmentor.org

www.helpmetothink.org

Please, let me know if you have any suggestion to improve this workbook as I want it to be useful for the majority of people.

Thank you in advance for your co-operation.